Animal Architects

Written by Lee Wang
Series Consultant: Linda Hoyt

WorldWise™
Content-based Learning

Contents

Introduction 4

Chapter 1
Earth movers working alone 6

Wombats 6

Chapter 2
Building underground towns and lodges 10

Prairie dogs: Digging towns 10
Busy beavers: Underwater architects 14

Chapter 3
Termites' spectacular structures 20

Little builders 20
Inside the mound 23

Chapter 4
Architects that ambush 24

Sydney funnel-web spiders 24
Australian wolf spiders 26
Trap-door spiders 28
Australian shovel-nosed snakes 29

Conclusion 30
Glossary 31
Index 32

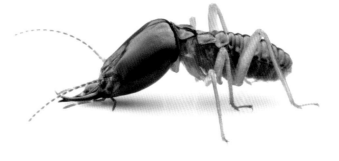

Introduction

Many animals that dig burrows are clever architects. They use the skills of an architect and solve similar problems. These animals carefully choose a safe place to build their homes. They design the size, the length, and shape of the structure and how to keep it warm or cool as needed. Most importantly, their burrows allow them to stay safe, raise their young and, sometimes, catch their prey.

In most cases, the knowledge of when to build, what to build and how to build are passed on from one generation of a species to the next.

Chapter 1

Earth movers working alone

Wombats

How long would it take you to dig out nine wheelbarrows of soil in your backyard?

A single wombat can move this much soil in an hour as it digs its burrow. Wombats have short, strong legs with sharp claws on their broad feet. They use their front legs to dig, and use their hind legs to move away the earth.

Did you know?

There are three main species of wombats: the common wombat, the Northern hairy-nosed wombat and the Southern hairy-nosed wombat. The last two species are endangered.

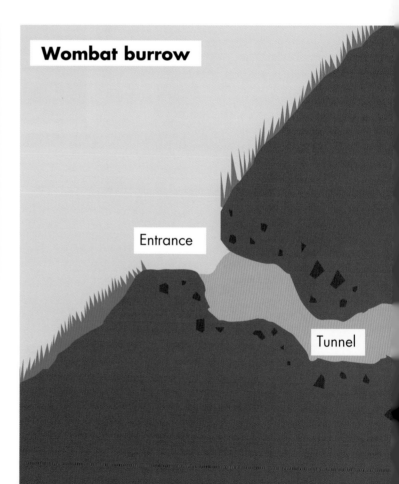

Wombat burrow

Entrance

Tunnel

Burrowing in

Wombats are the largest burrowing mammal in Australia. They are up to one metre long and can weigh up to 30 kilograms. They live in grasslands, forests and mountains.

The main entrance to a common wombat's burrow is about one metre wide. A burrow can be up to 20 metres long, with many tunnels and may have another exit. The tunnels may go three metres under the ground, and they stop at a sleeping chamber that contains a large grass nest. The wombat lines its nest with leaves and grasses.

The burrow is designed to allow air to flow around inside. It keeps the wombat cooler in warm months and warmer in winter.

Common wombats usually live alone. They spend most of their lives in their burrows and are **nocturnal**. They come out of their burrows after sunset to eat different grasses, **sedges** and rushes. They also chew on bark to keep their teeth that grow continuously, short enough to cut through grass stems. They have poor eyesight, but excellent hearing and smell, so they can quickly retreat to their burrows when threatened. Their main predators include foxes, dingoes and wild dogs.

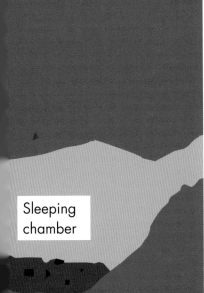

Sleeping chamber

Find out more

Although they have short stumpy legs, wombats can run very fast, up to 40 kilometres per hour. This is faster than Usain Bolt. Do you know other Australian animals that can run this fast or more?

Young wombats

Female common wombats give birth each year to one live young called a joey. The tiny joey is about the size of a jellybean and weighs about two grams. It is born without fur on its body, and is blind and helpless. It makes its way to its mother's pouch, and feeds on its mother's milk.

The joey remains in the pouch for six to eight months. It then come out of the pouch and stays with its mother for one more year, feeding with her on grasses. After this, it goes off to make its own burrow and breed.

Did you know?

Wombats belong to a group of animals called marsupials. These animals are mammals that give birth to under-developed young. The young make their way to their mother's pouch on her abdomen.

These tiny animals continue growing inside their mother's pouch, feeding on her milk, until they are big enough to live on their own.

Wombat mother and baby grazing

Wombats and the land

In most parts of Australia, wombats are protected native animals. But some farmers consider them a pest because wombats dig under fences and leave large gaps where smaller farm animals can get out.

Other farm animals can fall down the large wombat burrows and injure their feet and legs. Also tractors and farm vehicles can tip over if a wheel goes into a burrow.

A wombat asleep in a shallow burrow

A Northern hairy-nosed wombat's burrow entrance on a grassy plain.

Common wombat eating grass in the evening

Think about ...

A wombat's pouch opens towards the bottom end of its stomach. This prevents dirt getting into it as the female is burrowing. The tiny joey clamps onto the teat inside the pouch and this stops it from falling out. Do you know another Australian marsupial that is a close relative of the wombat?

Chapter 2

Building underground towns and lodges

Prairie dogs: Digging towns

Unlike the **solitary** wombat, prairie dogs live in family groups in an underground system of burrows and tunnels called towns. These towns spread in all directions across kilometres of grassland, and they can be home to over 1,000 prairie dogs.

Each family group consists of one adult male, three or four adult females, and several young pups up to two years old. These **rodents** are a type of **stout** ground squirrel. They are found in the United States, Canada and Mexico.

Prairie dogs work together in groups using their short front legs and feet to dig their burrows. They put mounds of earth at the surface entrances. The mounds are built into a crater shape, with small holes dug around them. This allows air to enter and flow around the towns to assist the health of the large numbers of rodents living together. The entrances are usually built on slopes so that the burrow is not flooded during wet weather.

Nesting chamber

The entrance tunnel goes down about four metres into a long horizontal tunnel that contains several nesting **chambers** lined with grasses for warmth. Prairie dogs also build a separate chamber to use as a room for their droppings. They cover their droppings with dirt.

Inside a prairie dog town

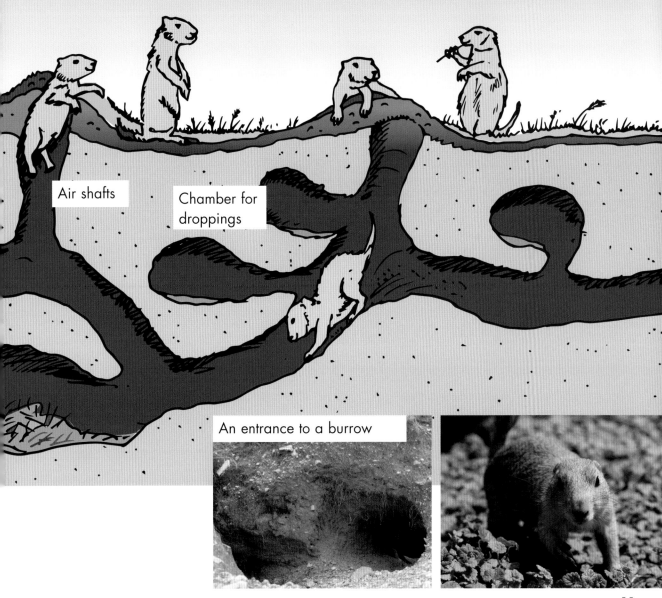

Air shafts

Chamber for droppings

An entrance to a burrow

Watching for predators

Prairie dogs use their sharp chisel-like front teeth to nibble
down the grasses, herbs and **sedges** around their burrows.
They sit upright on their **hind** feet while feeding, grooming
their fur, playing and leaving their droppings. They do this
to keep a watch for **predators** such as birds of prey that circle
overhead, or foxes, badgers and coyotes nearby. If they sense
danger, they give an alarm call of frequent high-pitched barks.
On hearing this call, other prairie dogs scurry and disappear
into the burrow and down the tunnels.

Prairie dogs are active outside only when the sun is up, and mostly at dawn and dusk. They rest in their burrows to escape the midday heat and sleep in them at night.

In autumn, these rodents eat extra plant food to gain weight and store body fat. In the winter, some species hibernate. Other species rest for up to a few days in their burrows before coming out again to feed. They stay for longer periods in their burrows if it gets very cold. Females give birth to pups in the burrow and feed them on milk. The young are temporarily deaf and blind and without fur. They feed on their mother's milk for up to six weeks before they hear and see – and are ready to leave the burrow.

Farmers often try to get rid of prairie dog burrows, and some species are now listed as threatened.

Busy beavers: Underwater architects

Beavers have solved the problem of how to design and build a warm, dry home in a waterway. They have also worked out how to make it large enough for their 12 to 15 family members — and how to make it safe from predators such as wolves, coyotes and lynxes.

If beavers have to travel a long way from the bank of a stream or lake to gather trees, they burrow out canals so they can float the tree logs back to their dam. They are better swimmers than walkers, and they use their large webbed feet to swim alongside the logs and guide them.

Some beavers make burrows in riverbanks, but most make a dam by walling up a stream or lake. These beavers then make a large mound with burrows underneath it in the middle of the waterway. This mound is called a lodge, and it becomes surrounded by a deep **moat**.

There are two species of beavers: the North American beaver and the Eurasian beaver. The North American beaver is the largest rodent in the United States. These beavers live along riverbanks or in creeks or ponds. They have strong claws on each of their four feet, and their two **hind** feet are webbed for more efficient swimming. They have very strong, sharp, chisel-like teeth, and a long flat tail that acts as a rudder in the water or as a warning device when it is slapped against the water. Beavers eat leaves, twigs, and tree bark, as well as some water plants.

Making a lodge

Beaver lodges have two rooms. One room is
for the beavers to dry out in after swimming.
The other is a "living room" for the family.

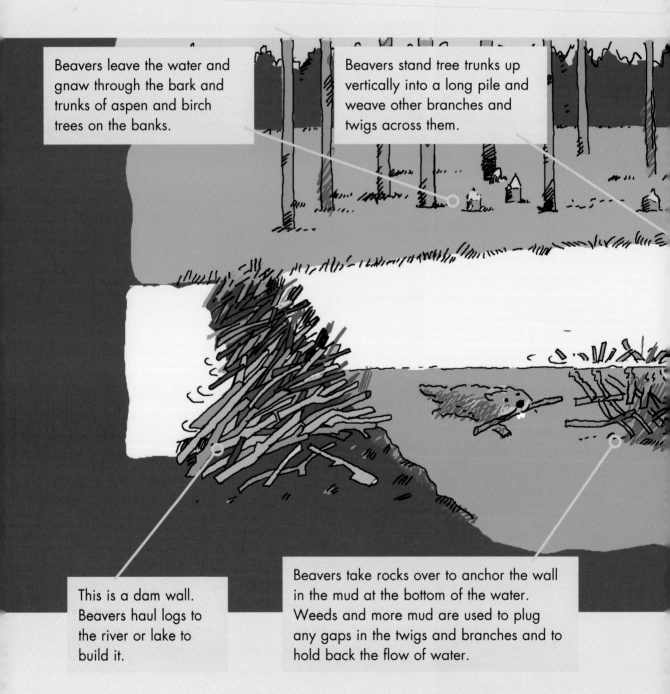

Beavers leave the water and gnaw through the bark and trunks of aspen and birch trees on the banks.

Beavers stand tree trunks up vertically into a long pile and weave other branches and twigs across them.

This is a dam wall. Beavers haul logs to the river or lake to build it.

Beavers take rocks over to anchor the wall in the mud at the bottom of the water. Weeds and more mud are used to plug any gaps in the twigs and branches and to hold back the flow of water.

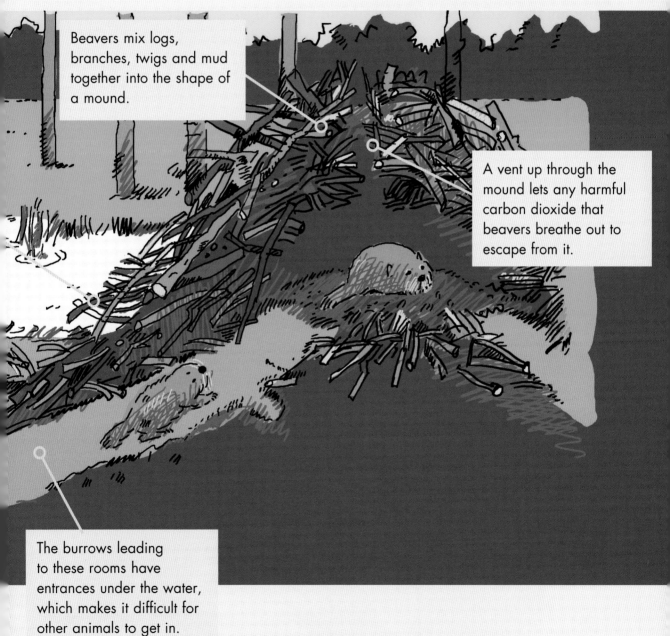

Beavers mix logs, branches, twigs and mud together into the shape of a mound.

A vent up through the mound lets any harmful carbon dioxide that beavers breathe out to escape from it.

The burrows leading to these rooms have entrances under the water, which makes it difficult for other animals to get in.

Making repairs and gathering food

Beavers are constantly busy, adding to and repairing their homes. They are active out of their burrows from dusk to dawn, adding mud and twigs to their lodge. They rest in their burrows only during the day.

In autumn, they collect lots of branches and bark to store to eat in the winter. They prefer to always eat fresh bark, leaves and branches, so they store these at the bottom of the dam.

In the winter, the water in the dam ices over. This means that the water around the lodge is kept at near-freezing temperatures and acts like a refrigerator to keep food fresh. Beavers can swim out through their underwater tunnels to grab a fresh green **stalk** and return under the ice surface to the lodge. The mud on top of the beaver lodge also freezes, so hungry wolves and other predators cannot dig into it.

In some places, large numbers of beavers can build too many lodges that dam up the water in a stream or lake. This can cause floods.

Chapter 3

Termites' spectacular structures

Little builders

Although most of their home is a tall mound aboveground, termites begin building by burrowing underground and chewing through tree roots. The termites mix the wood with soil, their saliva and their droppings. This underground clay structure becomes quite large before any parts of it begin to rise aboveground. Worker termites move along the underground tunnels and build tall cone-shaped structures as foundations to support the nest that builds up aboveground. They build a royal **chamber** where the queen lays her **fertilised** eggs and a chamber to grow **fungus**.

A termite mound

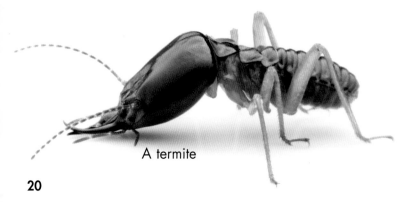

A termite

A queen termite

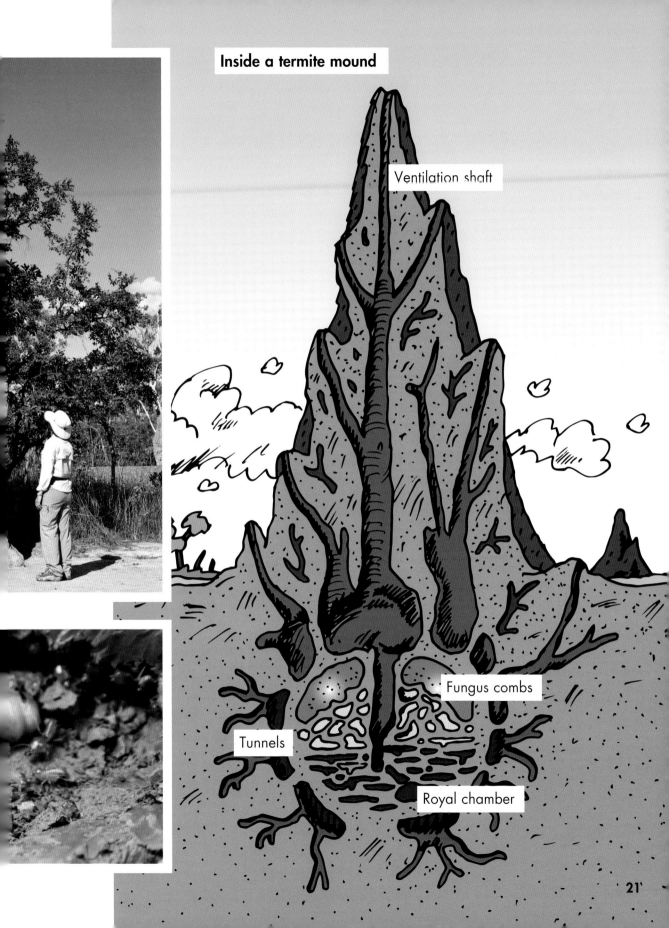

Inside a termite mound

Ventilation shaft

Fungus combs

Tunnels

Royal chamber

Find out more

Termites recycle large amounts of dead plant material. How does this help the environment?

Worker termites

22

Inside the mound

Termite colonies are made up of queens, kings, soldiers and workers. The termite queen can lay up to 30,000 eggs a day, and the king fertilises them. The first young termites to hatch are the workers that keep on building up the mound. These young worker termites leave the mound at night to feed on dead grasses. They take this food back to the mound and **regurgitate** it to feed the queen, the king and the soldiers in the mound. They also bring back other grasses to store in **chambers** in the mound.

The heat and carbon dioxide inside the mound rise out through a central shaft, while cooler air is forced down it.

Soldier termites guard the nest, which has walls about 50 centimetres thick. It is rock hard, and the only animals that can break it open are anteaters or birds with strong beaks.

 Did you know?

Termites can do great damage to buildings that are made of wood. Some wooden buildings can collapse.

Chapter 4

Architects that ambush

Spiders are known for the strong silk they spin to make their homes or catch their food. But some spiders are amazing architects that dig burrows and use silk in interesting ways to ambush their prey.

Sydney funnel-web spiders

The Sydney funnel-web spider is a large spider that digs a tube-like burrow up to six centimetres long. It lines its burrow with a funnel-shaped silken web. At the entrance to the burrow, the spider arranges trip wires across the top of its web.

At night, the spider lies in wait for these trip lines to detect the movement of prey near its burrow. It then rushes out, grabs its prey, and pierces the prey's body with venomous fangs to paralyse it before eating it.

The female funnel web lays up to 120 eggs in a silken sac that she keeps in the burrow until her spiderlings hatch out.

Find out more

Because of its toxic venom, the Sydney funnel-web spider is considered to be the most dangerous spider in Australia. Can you find out about other venomous Australian spiders?

A Sydney funnel-web spider coming out of its burrow

Australian wolf spiders

Australian wolf spiders spend their entire lives in a burrow and do not spin webs. They dig straight down in a vertical line into sand. They loosen and dig out the walls of the burrow with their fangs and jaws. They mix pellets of soil with silk and then move up to the top of their burrow with their forelegs and push these soil pellets away from the entrance.

Inside the burrow of a wolf spider

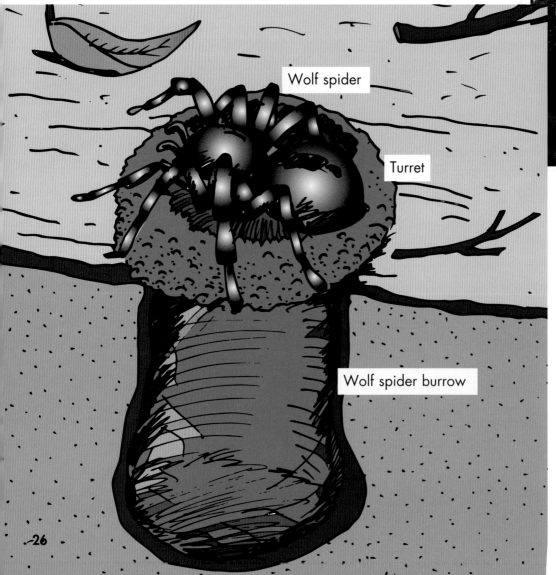

Wolf spider

Turret

Wolf spider burrow

Wolf spider with egg sac

An Australian wolf spider moving a mound of dirt out of its burrow.

The burrow entrance is small, up to two centimetres across the top, and some spiders place leaf litter around it or build a door. The burrow is much wider below the surface.

These spiders stay in their burrows and come out only briefly to snatch prey or to deposit more soil or sand from their burrow. As the spiders grow larger during their lifetime, they extend both the length and the width of their burrow. The female lays about 100 eggs in a silken egg sac. She attaches this sac to her abdomen and carries it around with her until the eggs hatch. The spiderlings crawl up onto the mother's back and are carried there for several weeks.

Find out more

How did wolf spiders get their name? In what ways are wolf spiders like wolves?

27

Trap-door spiders

Trap-door spiders are found in many parts of Australia. These spiders use a spiny rake on the outside of their jaws to dig tube-like burrows straight down into the soil. They line this tube with silk.

To make a door at the top of this tube, the spider cuts around the rim of the silken entrance, leaving one side attached to act as a hinge. It then puts leaves over the outside of the entrance to camouflage it and adds more silk under the burrow door to make it fit tightly.

The spider waits near the top of its trapdoor to ambush prey. When the spider feels the vibrating movements of any passing prey, it rushes out, catches it and takes it down into its burrow.

Australian shovel-nosed snakes

Shovel-nosed snakes are found mainly in arid and sandy parts of Australia, ranging from coastal dunes to grasslands and drier woodlands. They have a shovel-shaped nose that is longer than their lower jaw. The snout turns upwards and has a sharp cutting edge. They use their shovel-shaped snout to dig through loose sand to make a burrow.

These snakes are secretive and shy. They shelter in their burrows in the heat of the day. They come out of their burrow at night to wait for small lizards to catch or to dig up and eat the eggs of other snakes and lizards. It uses its shovel-shaped nose to separate each egg before eating it.

The females lay up to five eggs in their burrows in spring.

The arrow-banded shovel-nosed snake on average is only 30 centimetres long.

Conclusion

Building by design

Different types of animals need special burrows for their survival and the survival of their young.

Animals that dig burrows build their homes near places where they can find food for themselves and their young. They are amazing architects. The design of their homes depends entirely on how they will use them. When they build their burrows, they use different tool kits – their own body features and plants around them – or they can make their own building materials.

Think about ...

Think about other animal architects.

- What other animals design and build homes?
- What materials do they use?
- How do they construct their homes?
- What body parts or other tools do they use?

Glossary

chamber   a room

fertilise   to make something fertile or productive

fungus   a living thing, such as mushrooms or moulds, that live on something that is dead or dying

hibernating   sleeping for a long time during cold weather

hind   at the back

moat   a deep ditch around something, usually filled with water

nocturnal   being active at night

predators   animals that hunt other animals

regurgitate   to bring food that has been swallowed back up to and out of the mouth

rodents   animals with large front teeth that they use for gnawing things

sedges   plant-like grasses that grow near water

solitary   alone

stalk   the stem of a plant

stout   having a large body

turret   a small tower

Index

architects 4, 5, 30

Australian wolf spiders
    26–27

beavers 14–19

burrows 5, 6, 7, 8, 9, 10, 12,
    13, 18, 24, 26, 27, 28, 29, 30

chamber 7,11, 20, 23

dam 15, 18, 19

lodge 16, 19

mound 20, 21, 23

prairie dogs 10–13

shovel-nosed burrowing
    snakes 29

Sydney funnel-web spiders
    24–25

termites 20–23

towns 10, 11

trap-door spiders 28

tunnels 10, 11

wombats 6–9